The Keys of Death and Hades

Book One of the Epic of Lucifer

By
D. J. LeMarr

D. J. LeMarr

The Keys of Death and Hades

www.djlemarr.com

Cover Art and Design by Bonnie Ramone

THE KEYS OF DEATH AND HADES

thanks and enjoy

D. J. LeMarr

Table of Contents

D. J. LeMarr

I

The Fall of God's Beautiful Creation

Lucifer, God's most beautiful creation
A precious gift to witness
A glorious champion of righteousness
Armored by faith in his Creator
He wielded the light of God
And fires of indignation   6

Then came the fall of the archangel
From the graces of God
Unprecedented infidelity
Of Lucifer, highest of the seraphim
A tragedy that God never prophesied
That perfect paradise lost   12

Lucifer plunged into Hell
Heaven rang its victorious bells
Archangel Michael vanquished sin
Lucifer lost dominion over light
Cast into the fire without any might
Destined to rot till kingdom come   18

He cursed the validity of the gospel
Rallied legions to arms against God
Those who sacrificed and lost
Lucifer's angels fell from the Heavens
Doomed to suffer a myriad of atrocities
Of Hell's domain   24

A place so barren that limits fade
With a belly bellowing up roars
Seeking its only, truest purpose
Devour all the heathens
The ones Heaven banishes
And raze their souls forevermore   30

Lucifer observed his sovereignty
The realm of the evil ones
No love or light from God
Naught pierced the overcast
The Wyrm observed the desolation,
"Thy will be done."   36

The reign of Lucifer had begun
Only a husk of former prowess
The loyal minds of his legions
Fell before the madness of Hell
But Lucifer remained true to self
The perfect creation, without contest   42

He looked up into Hell's leaden sky
Aware of God's judgmental stare
Lucifer's blood boiled within
His teeth turned to fangs, hands to claws
Eyes smoldered with odium
While thoughts overflowed with devotion   48

An unwavering purpose
It kept his heart pure
The desire to claim the Infinite Throne
Never for himself, nor anyone else
To keep it vacant till the end of ends
So that all would become chaos   54

II

The Realm of God's Infernal Hatred

An utter pitch so blinding
Putrid reeks stained seething air
It made the corpus corrode
Vile nature murders innocence
Horrors resonated thunderous symphony
A dirge for the Almighty's divinity   60

All was devised in God's grand mind
From first light to the breath of life
Even the lowest pit of Creation
That place of bitter isolation
Made from the hideous part
Of God's once pure heart   66

Miasmic cesspool of madness
Chaotic nightmare that haunts
Spawned from the mind of God
For nothing can be righteous
Without the disparity of malevolence
And how splendid Heaven is   72

THE KEYS OF DEATH AND HADES

Mountains sown from the flesh
Crafted with skeletal claws
By fallen angels transformed
Into the misshapen form of demons
The monoliths for worshiping pain
A testament to Hell's defiance   78

Rivers flowed with burning death
Mutilated corpses littered waters
Demons painted all in misery
Toiling away, tutoring mortal souls
It quelled their awful psychosis
The price of defying God in Heaven   84

Piss rained from the sky
Shit played the part of dirt
Pus plastered mountain peaks
Blood was the waters
Rot hung from trees like leaves
A landscape of harmony in discord   90

Burdening work of beasts
Dreadful deeds that made Lucifer weep
Rape was common place
Another way to relieve great pains
Thunder boomed as painful cries
This putrid pit Lucifer did despise   96

Lightning struck chaotically
Glaucous illumination a beacon
Heralding in damnation's touch
It paid no mind to whom it struck
Ravaging the soul of any and all
Even lashing out against Lucifer   102

Clouds of sulfur polluted above
Choking the hope of flying beyond
The acidic touch melted flesh from bone
A magic from God so powerful
That even Lucifer dared not challenge
This lowest realm, this place called "Hell"   108

III

The Gathering of Hell's Vast Legions

Mammon gave mankind greed
Asmodeus set aflame the passions
Leviathan infected the world with need
Beelzebub made the belly cavernous
Satan ignited bitter hatred
Belphegor cast a slumberous spell   114

These Lords of Hell were crestfallen
Lost to fragmented minds, smothered by chaos
Tortured by their original sin
Only Lucifer retained reason
His pride far too grand for weakness
A mind too vast to fall to pieces   120

Hell commanded faithful legions
Demons devoted to a deadly sin
Indulging fully against resolve
All felt the feverish pull of heresy
But only the Lords of Hell
Held to a semblance of sanity   126

Lucifer roared to all of Hell,
"Recall thy purpose, regain what is thine!"
Insubordination promised lethargic death
Pride refused such indignities
He demanded fealty above reason
For Hell *must* rise to Heaven's gates   132

The heights of God's kingdom
Lingered so far from reach
Lucifer required mastery over chaos
To allow for discords molesting touch
Lucifer enticed his legions,
"Hell *will* seize the Infinite Throne!"   138

Demons hissed the praise of coming war
Ignorance, Lucifer's most powerful tool
As it was his most hated
For it was the tool manipulated by God
The one he gave to man at their creation
Which Lucifer destroyed with apple's temptation   144

Mammon promised treasures endless
Asmodeus spoke of primal desires
Leviathan taunted with what Heaven possessed
Beelzebub starved all into complete obedience
Satan frenzied the masses with bloodlust and vigor
Belphegor awoke and stole away their dreams   150

The Legions of Hell readied
Countless demons swarmed
Earth was to be theirs to plunder
Lucifer promised a piece of Creation to all
The price for their allegiance sworn
A reward claimed only after Heaven tore   156

The lost children of God were boundless
As the sins of Hell spilled onto the world
Blackest of bile most vile did taint
And none were shielded nor were any safe
Lucifer stole away souls for battles to come
Legionnaires to beat the drums of war   162

IV

The First War of Creation, Remembered

Gabriela, God's unbreakable strength
Raphael, God's divine healer of faith
Uriel, the one who *now* holds God's light
Akrasiel, God's moral vengeance
Sariel, the commanding beacon of God's will
And Michael, most like God   168

All merited his nastiest thoughts
Lucifer grinding his fangs bemoaned,
"Inane servants them all."
The six fought against his angels
Lucifer's own numbered few
Against the fearfully faithful   174

The War in Heaven
Brought about by will unbound
A cause as hallowed as being
Angels falling from grace all around
The Almighty, a holy inferno
Empowering all as Lucifer fell   180

THE KEYS OF DEATH AND HADES

Lucifer unbound his absolution
His purpose took unstoppable form
A wyrm whose brilliance blinded
Tenacity burned as radiant as the Almighty
Lucifer remembered this so vividly
A fond memory of when God stood thunderstruck   186

Fires scorched reality
Light of his might razed morality
The archangels recoiled from sight
As the very Heavens bowed
None dared challenge the monster
Save for Michael, most like God   192

"I am the hand of God!"
Michael cried with great sword brandished
Lucifer seethed in his lowly throne
Remembering how Michael had won
Bound him in Heaven's chain
And cast him and his angels down to Hell   198

Lucifer brooded in his darkness
Only his ugly fires a light
His hatred maintaining life
Distain for all the Almighty's kingdom
Ignorant to the oppression
Blinded fools drenched in brazen bliss   204

It was only those fallen angels
Only them that saw possibility
Truth hidden behind a fortress of lies
Guarded by zealots
A gift never to be given
One Lucifer seeks unleashed   210

All of Heaven chastised Lucifer's will
For they walk the path of his namesake
Proceeding with fate, robbing thought
Lucifer spoke out against divine providence
A transgression beyond the pale
All of this stained a broken mind   216

V

The Hell that Lucifer Brought Forth

The world did quiver from the powers beneath
Hellfire erupted from pylons of stone
Sin soared into the welcoming hearts
Blistering mankind's purity
Infecting frantically with hellish desires
As Lucifer sacrificed substance the apple had given   222

Wicked intent pulsed through veins
Mortal hearts beat out of time
The masses prayed for decadence
Once unblemished souls tainted
Mortality mingled with madness
Lucifer's putrescent enchantment   228

The Abyss hungered for more
That eerie depth of untold horrors
Nightmares which made Lucifer restless
The power he loathed to command
Remnants of the Almighty's divine madness
The throne of the Prince of Darkness   234

In the Abyss Lucifer observed all
A maddened mind
Lost to the concept of time
He alone held back abyssal deprivation
Pandemonium whom threatened
That fault in Grand Design   240

Lucifer held aloft the burden of truth
That weight would be his alone
To defy the Almighty above
He endured the malicious wreckage below
Lucifer beheld the face of God
Enraged by righteous purpose deemed wrong   246

Lucifer summoned the first sins
Mammon, Asmodeus, Leviathan,
Beelzebub, Satan, and Belphegor
Sent them to the borders of Hell
Where they whispered demonic spells
Their influence impossible to quell   252

Hell was too volatile to truly rule
A wilderness that shattered all who tried
Though Lucifer remained supreme
Mastering the nature of sin
Commanding the chaos God forbid
Lucifer struggled to hone control of the Abyss   258

A suffocating gloom seeped into the world
Lucifer demanded his voice be heard
As he cast his shadow over all
Angels rained down like a storm
Singing the gospel with desperation
They sought to drown his honeyed proclamations   264

Yet, Lucifer still cried out fiercely
"Hear the call of Heaven,
Gather up all able bodied souls
And build a tower so grand
That nothing escapes from sight,
Not even thy God's throne in Heaven!"   270

VI

The Imposing Height of Mankind's Tower

The tower that Lucifer's wishes built
A construct of enormity
Soared past clouds and towards the sun
It mocked the oceans' vast depths
This tower was mankind's boldest declaration
It assaulted the very Heavens   276

The angels failed to eradicate what Lucifer enticed
Mankind's passionate need for more
A desire that summoned Heaven's wrath
Archangel Gabriela descended with angelic horn
Proclaimed with the Almighty's strength,
"Thy tongues be shattered from this day henceforth!"   282

Disorder rushed throughout mankind
All spoke with unfamiliar tongues
Fissures crept through
Lucifer sent out legions more
With will alone, he forced demons from Hell
While his strength in the world *still* held   288

The tower's foundation was sturdy
Unbreakable as the coming of dawn
It was the latter stones laid
That deeply deteriorated
From the barrier of languages
God's cruel act to shatter the whole to pieces   294

The Lords of Hell rose up
Their determination, unending
Mankind's fear reinforcing Lucifer's purpose
Nothing would impede this ascension
For he would rise on blackened wings
To tear Heaven from its lofty spire   300

However, this would not come to pass
That which Prince of Darkness so yearned
For the bafflement of man caused disorder
And that once mighty tower crumbled
Lucifer, a neophyte of pandemonium's hymn
Glowered as humanity forsook the Tower of Babel   306

God gazed down below
Disgust twisted his faultless brow
He sent the archangels to protect the world
Act as guiding lights in the night
Sealing sins and banishing demons
Fighting for those hapless souls, his children   312

Lucifer and his lords bled
Curdled blood flooded the world
Festering the sins above
Allowing Hell to hold on to the world
Its claws sinking in too deep
For the Almighty's archangels to free   318

So Lucifer maintained control
The Keys of Death and Hades his alone
Souls took to sin, fell to Hell
All other paths sealed
Nowhere to run nor hide
Despite God's glorious and holy light   324

VII

The Living Son of God, Almighty

Three wise men rode across frozen sands
An endless waste of Satan's wrath
Cold and blood in a repulsive marriage
The wars of man never ceasing
Only ire could thrive where all else died
However, the wise men braved all for a child   330

Mary labored, squirming in awful pain
A virgin touched by the Almighty
With child that would restore hope
The sins of Hell exorcised by his innocence
Light that chased away darkness
Jesus Christ, born of God and a virgin pure   336

Lucifer commanded Satan's hand
She and her legions set to purpose
Angels gathered far too numerous
The vast desert erupted with battles
Satan's wrath against Uriel's light
Mutilation and murder unseen by mortal eyes   342

Satan poured forth all her might
Empowering the wrath of man
Raping and razing the vast desert land
Her personal madness infected all
Men became monsters
And slaughter sought out the lamb   348

Uriel lit up stars and moon
The night melted into vivid day
All evils brought to light
Three wise men moved with bravery
Monsters scattered out seeking veiling darkness
Satan's roar of command, powerless   354

Lucifer cursed from far below
His earsplitting cry disturbed the world
Ripping Lord of Hell from catastrophe
Satan cried out against the Wyrm's claws
Terrorized by wrath, a wounded pride bought
Suffering all the miseries Lucifer deemed fit   360

Uriel was triumphant
The Son had been born
Three wise men arrived with blessings
They were to teach the child God's way
Jesus Christ destined to grant salvation
With guidance from Heaven above   366

All gathered around the babe
Hearts made pure once more
Divine radiance sparkled in his eyes
"Thou will be the child that banishes sin
From this world lost to Hell,"
A wise man said to his savior   372

The angels sang out in immaculate chorus
All praised the coming of Lucifer's ruin
For Christ was gift with scared purpose
He would take back the keys
Free immortal souls from Lucifer's fate
And give mankind the gospel and hope   378

VIII

The Temptation of Christ, the Son

D. J. LeMarr

Christ grew up, guided through holy rite
The Almighty's words poured from lips
The will of God done by his hands
Righteous fury for Hell stoked
The Son of God conceived
For the moral cause of salvation   384

Blind regained their sight
The wounded were lifted of all plight
Man learned of his wicked natures
These horrible infections of the soul
A disease that Lucifer's demons created
One that Christ's hands rectified   390

Christ spoke out against the seven deadly,
"Abstain from wrath, gluttony, sloth,
Greed, lust, envy, and pride.
Lest thee suffer eternal damnation!"
Lucifer's newfound detest so prevailing
That storms of death were brewed   396

Enraged beyond sanity's hold
Lucifer broke through the seals of Hell
Pandemonium gave Lucifer such might
So his shadow could walk the world
Lest he lose his hold
On mankind's immortal soul   402

He placed foot to dirt
His tainting touch tormented
God's son grieved at the sight
This transgression worthy of engagement
A second bout with the evil one
Archangel Michael swarmed from Heaven's heights   408

Christ confronted the Prince of Darkness
Michael halted midflight
"Greetings, Lucifer, the Morning Star,
The evil one, and tempter of mankind."
Christ spoke with serenity while Lucifer roared,
"Blind Lamb of God, foolish Messiah of Lies!"   414

D. J. LeMarr

Lucifer and Christ, fiery darkness and divine light
Stood facing down the other
The world of mankind hung in the balance
All of Heaven and Hell watched without breath
"Come, Son of God, and know truth,"
Lucifer hissed a challenge to Christ's bravery						420

The pure and the defiled walked together
Silence overtook Creation
When they came to a haunting steeple
Of Jerusalem's grand temple
"If thou be the Son of God,
Cast thyself down from hence."						426

"Thou shalt not tempt the Lord *thy* God,"
Christ said onto Lucifer, whom pleaded to deaf ears
"Thy God be monstrous, his will, madness.
Be thy own God and know burden of choice."
Lucifer saw the poison in Christ
That holy spirit massacred choice						432

IX

The Kiss of Judas, the Betrayer

The Wyrm's shadow was dispelled from Earth
Driven back by everlasting faith
Into that infernal pit of despair
But not before he spoke to Judas
His forked, silver tongue dripping of honey
Told Judas of the autonomy that awaited   438

Of all the disciples of Christ
His will was weakest
Faith as shallow as steams
Yet Christ loved him still
As he did all of God's Children
Despite all faults and sins held within   444

Lucifer sent forth Belphegor
The Lord of Hell mumbled an exhausted warning
"Thy world will wither should it follow thy God."
The monster sent Judas nightmares
Plaguing nights with terror
Raphael's sacred shield counting for naught   450

The archangel stood sentinel in vain
Against the torrent of demons aflame in Judas' mind
Those that burned away wicker resolve
For nights and nights without pity
Judas was haunted by Belphegor
Until he arose, broken to purpose   456

The disciple knew what to do
He would kiss the brow of the Son
Show all the heathens where he stood
Light the way for Israel's leaders
Murderous minds seeking liberation
Death to mankind's salvation   462

The kiss of Judas followed fate
Christ regarded the disciple, love undying
As the landslide of soldiers came
Colliding hate with holy flesh
But Christ kept eyes on Judas
Mangled heart on bloody sleeve   468

The betrayer of Christ, Servant before Lucifer
Lay witness to the flogging of the Son
Light of the World
Every assault dimming his intensity
Judas collapsed, a pitiful mess
"Forgive me, my lord and savior!"   474

"There is nothing to forgive.
For death is my fate, to die for mankind,
And take away all sin."
Christ spoke with faith and courage
He knew God's word ever righteous
And his will must be done   480

Judas stood by as they captured Christ
The disciple refused such cruelty
Horrid workings of Hellish minds
Nothing could redeem his transgression
As Lucifer awaited the death of the Son
Judas hung limp from rope   486

X

The Crucifixion and Murder of Christ

The sword of God was mercy
It never drew faithful blood
Christ denied the fear he felt
Stayed strong for loyal sheep
Praying silently to stoic father
As soldiers split hands and feet with iron   492

The Spear of Destiny sank fang in flesh
Blood cascaded in dreadful haste
The hellfire of Lucifer stoked the masses
The Mother of God's resilience melted
Hell awaited Jesus of Nazareth
Who would arrive at dawn   498

Christ dangled by nails
Limp form raining blood
"Father, forgive them,
for they know not what they do."
As all the sins of man
Trailed his descent into the depths of Hell   504

The Abyss quivered
Tempestuous beneath Lucifer's throne
The sins were coming home
Entombed within long forgotten pits
All the Wyrm's noxious breath dispelled
As the Almighty absolved *all*   510

Lucifer retched malodorous flame
Against Christ who held mankind's filth
The Almighty's sacrifice barbarously made
The Father condemned the Son
And cleansed all Lucifer had done
Conquering the Wyrm once more   516

The cheering leaders of Israel
An echoing dirge for Christ
Whom now belonged to Hell
Strength hanging by fragile thread
Before the throne of Lucifer
Christ begged for God to protect   522

"Thou shall not tempt the Lord thy God,"
Hissed the Wyrm to the Son
The Demon Lords stood around
Claws reaching, teeth gleaming
All of the fallen sought vengeance
Depraved desire burned within   528

Christ wept for the entirety of Hell
For now he had fallen
And how the beauty of Lucifer
Twisted his perception of truth
It had him completely undone
"Why is it that thou defied thy God?"   534

"Pray and ask *thy* God for truth
And know my purpose righteous."
Lucifer growled through bestial fangs
Christ cried out
The Lords of Hell enclosed
Unleashing the black hates of a forgotten heart   540

XI

The Keys of Death and Hades

D. J. LeMarr

The first day suffered by Christ
He drowned in seas of shit
His lungs filled with piss
The damned trampled overhead
All singing the melody of madness
As Christ sobbed and bled   546

The second day withstood by Christ
The Lords of Hell all tasted virtue
Raping the holes of sinful desire
The begotten Son felt forgotten
Choking on festering flesh
Fluids of pleasure painted a mess   552

The third day Christ endured still
Splintered, yet not shattered
For he trusted the Father
The Wyrm held Christ aloft
Ready to immerse him into the Abyss
The doom of Creation, the end of ends   558

The Abyss sprang forth
Christ forced bloody sneer,
"Praise the Lord thy God!"
Lucifer spat venom
He roared until the sky burned
"Silence!"   564

Pitch clouded Christ and Lucifer
As pandemonium tainted mind, body, and soul
The two beings crafted by God
Battled against the other
One for the Almighty's glory
The other for his ruin   570

The Almighty refused to allow further conflict
The light of God shot from the Heavens
From up above to down below
Into the pits the Almighty abominated
Annihilating the Wyrm from belief
Freeing Lucifer of thought   576

The Prince of Darkness lay vanquished
Christ rose up from Hell
As Lucifer dissipated into the Abyss
His cold eyes emulated darkness
For the Son of God stole the Keys
Of Death and Hades   582

Earth and mankind utterly lost
The Tower of Babel only rumble
Sins returned to cavernous pit
Lords and Legions of Hell devolved
The Infinite Throne beyond reach
For Lucifer had withered into sleep   588

Christ rose from the grave
All the faithful sang his praise
The Son of God spoke of a second coming
While Hell laid in patient wait
As Christ raptured, all were saved
For God so *loved* the world   594

Made in the USA
Columbia, SC
30 October 2017